Openings 35
The Poetry Society of the Open University

Annual Anthology

of

OU Poets

2018

Copyright remains with the individual poets.
All rights reserved.

Published 2018 by Open University Poets.

ISBN 978-0-9567833-6-3

Editor: Sue Spiers
Cover: Looking Happy by Parastoo Ganjei
Printed by Lulu.com

Introduction

OU Poets is the Poetry Society of the Open University. It is open to any student or staff member, past or present. At the time of going to press there are about 80 members from all over the U.K. with some in mainland Europe and worldwide.

Members of the society submit poems to a magazine, which is produced 5 times a year, each one having a different voluntary editor. The magazine is not a publication *per se* and is strictly produced by the members for the members. There is a section for comment and criticism of members' work.

At the end of the year, members are asked to vote for the 20 poems they most appreciated from the 5 magazines produced that year. Those with the most votes, allowing for no more than one poem per poet, appear in the following year's issue of Openings. The anthology is as broad-based as the society itself and reflects the varied backgrounds, interests and tastes of the members.

If you would like more information about OU Poets, please contact the Secretary:

>Adrian Green
>Flat 3
>1 Clifton Terrace
>Southend-on-Sea
>SS1 1DT
>adrian@greenad.co.uk

or visit our website at http://www.oupoets.org.uk

 Facebook   Twitter

Contents

Nineteen Fifties Milk Teeth	Alan Durham	6
December	Katherine Rawlings	7
Donna Nook	Ross McGivern	8
Our Last Goodbye	Phil Craddock	9
A Vanishing	Onno Tromp	10
Coda	Kewal Paingankar	11
Down Pudding Lane	Hilary Mellon	12
The Old Machete	Mark Bones	13
Waking at Six in Sicily	Cate Cody	14
Oink!	Susan Jarvis Bryant	15
A Traitor to Moonlight	Chris McCaffrey	16
When Comes the Spring?	Barrie Williams	17
Why I Don't Like Roses	Liz Rowlands	18
Thimble	Julie Stamp	19
The Christmas Present	Jenny Hamlett	20
A Prisoner of Form	Lem Ibbotson	21
Love Poem for Chris	Ian Campbell	22
Bolton Palais Saturday Night 1960	Sally James	24
For Her... Later...	Sally Charnock	25
Looks Like Strange Weather	Vicki Morley	26

Contents

Going South	Stacey Lane	27
From the Cliff Gardens	Adrian Green	28
Exquisite Corpses	Andrew W. Pye	30
Turning Point	Denis Ahern	32
A Lifetime of Loving	Sylvia Armstrong	33
Perspectives	Rose Docherty	35
Wmbldn	John Starbuck	36
Political Tennis	Bernard Rooney	37
Empty Nest	Nigel Kent	38
The Broad Highway	K. J. Barrett	40
Rosebay Willowherb	Barbara Cumbers	41
Homage to Mondrian	Polly Stretton	42
Woman with a Niqab...	Eric Karoulla	43
Married by the Book	Alice Harrison	44
Aubade	Jacob Lund	45
Now, and Then	Helen Harvey	46
28th June 1928	Jim Lindop	48
Classified Ad: Runner Wanted	Julie Anne Gilligan	49
How I Learned to 'B'	Sue Spiers	50
To My Son	Rosa Thomas	51

Alan Durham

Nineteen Fifties Milk Teeth

Our milkman had a yellow skin,
he had no flesh, he was so thin.
Every day he stopped to chat,
especially to our hostile cat.

His mouth all broke, his jaw askew,
a smile so warm and words so few.
He had a limp, his ribs stuck out,
he looked like no one else about.

'Mam! Is Co-op George Chinese?'
'No! He's as English as you please.'
'But he looks so ill and his teeth have gaps.'
'It was the blasted war and the cruel Japs.'

Katherine Rawlings

December

Through a morning mist
Drizzle snivels on the windows
The sun cringing in pale retreat
Birds gone to winter in the South
Weather reports are grim
Under a relentless Arctic blast
The sea heaves bronchially
Tosses on its bed as might a sick patient
Overhead I hear
Seagulls fleeing inland to a nearby river
Sluggish with Seasonal Affected Disorder
Shivering squirrels hibernate
In the trunks of sullenly skeletal trees
Yet December has festivities
Lights and tinsel and song
In January the worst is yet to come
Until the snowdrops appear

Ross McGivern

Donna Nook

The North Sea echoes, echoes
in and out, out,
and in, in laboured time. Time
stops at the dunes. The dunes
song; a wailing moan, a wailing moan
for a lost child. A lost child's
cry that pulsates, pulsates
through anchored gorse. Gorse
buffets and rocks, and rocks
itself to sleep in the cradle, the cradle
of the North Sea as it echoes, echoes
through time and place. And this place,
is where they've come to be heard. Heard
above the crashing groans. Crashing groans
and breakers hit, hit
mud flats and vanish, and vanish
until they muster up another gulp, another gulp
of air that spews spray over the Herd. The herd
of Seals birthing, birthing
in clumps of sea-grass and pups. Pups
honking for food. For food,
for a mother's love on a plain, a plain
of life and death. Life and death
blown in on the North Sea echoes, echoes
in and out, out and in, in laboured time.

Phil Craddock

Our Last Goodbye

There were rain clouds racing and storm-blown leaves
on the day we last said goodbye
and you turned away and you didn't look back
and I cried, O Love, did I cry.

There were opened presents and left-over drinks
and balloons that yearned for the sky
and I knew I couldn't persuade you to stay
though I tried, O God, did I try.

And every year, at this time of year
when the cold wind calls down the hall
I always hear what I'm wanting to hear
though I know it's no-one at all.

I will wait forever, the whole of time,
my tears will never run dry,
for I love you still as I loved you then
when we goodbyed our last goodbye.

Onno Tromp

The Not So Great: A Vanishing

They can see
your shoe laces
need tying

"Tired,
grubby,
and rather smelly"

not that
they can see
nothingness

after all
they can see
your shoe laces
need tying

Kewal Paigankar

Coda

You talked about angles and curves
I chipped in with contours and spaces
You'd discuss prologues and preambles
When the nights closed in;
I'd counter with epilogues and postscripts.
You loved interludes and breaks
I preferred intermissions and intervals
You had your rhymes and verses
I had rhythm and stanzas.

Your bacchanalian spirit;
It was wild and uninhibited.
I had days of hedonism
But they were moderate,
Not laced with your excess.
You were a nocturnal vixen
By turns intemperate and capricious.
My self-restraint and equanimity
Cowered and quivered before your gale force.

The inevitable break-up;
You called it a mere hiatus and an impasse.
For me it was terminal and final,
Every moment a dread.
Irreconcilable differences.

Hilary Mellon

Down Pudding Lane

The bleak remains of drunken fights
hung over by these churchyard trees
lie here – where shadows can't conceal
what rags of sunlight now reveal
– detritus only daylight sees
and evidence of summer nights

Mark Bones

The Old Machete

Barely a tap
from the dark blade of the old machete,
and a sweet flake shivers and falls
from the meat
of the wood that will feed the flame,
and begins its task of scenting the house before
another fire can be born
to lie like a whispered prayer,
in the cupped palm of the grate.

> Taps from an old blade.
> Slivers of filleted wood.
> Flames licking their fill.

Surely this blade itself was carved,
from ironwood.
It eases the flesh of the sapling apart,
and settles to feed without any fuss.
Always the dutiful predator,
suckling its young,
before it can sleep.

> Are those their eyes,
> aglow in the dark?

Cate Cody

Waking at Six in Sicily

Waking at six in Sicily
Dark, smoky, charcoal-grey clouds
Sit heavy but unthreatening,
Above them a thin line of lemon sky
Topped with cream and vast vats of blue

Below the charcoal, two layers
Of fiery, ripe coral
And silver-grey,
Meet the crust of an indigo sea.

The lights from the town in front
Pour out below,
Sparkling like the embers of Etna

Dark green shadows from our own olive trees
Form the rocky base of our morning volcano.

Susan Jarvis Bryant

Oink!

I wandered lonely as a pig
who's shunned from sty and starved of swill.
Those runts who didn't give a fig
can shove a jocund daffodil
towards a wink of twinkling sky
where they will see this porker fly.

And float I will o'er vale and hill;
I'll gloat above the grunting fray.
While Venus lights my porcine thrill,
I'll glide the moon-kissed Milky Way
and snort at each notorious boar;
such glorious hogs are born to soar.

Scornful swine with no remorse
can douse themselves in apple sauce!

Chris McCaffrey

A Traitor to Moonlight

I've watched you pass for countless years,
Beneath my glow in peaceful dark,
With flawless rhythmic spins and arcs:
My only earth, my mother sphere.

Now drowning in a traitor's light,
You're screeching like opposing gears
Which grind against your stainless tears;
Corroding under manmade blight.

It's raping every gasp of air,
Ravaging every inch of meat,
Extracting all your healthy teeth,
Pillaging every strand of hair,

For oil and gas; for bombs and blood;
For poisoned lochs; for blackened earth;
For rubble mounds; for grief and death;
For scorching heat; for storms and floods.

I'll watch you pass with countless tears,
Collapsing under manmade blight,
My glow dethroned by manmade light;
My only earth, my mother sphere.

Barrie Williams

When Comes the Spring?

You ask, When's Spring? There's those who say
When night no more exceeds the day.
When we get up at dawn's first light
And not too soon shut out the night.

But others say, First day of March –
Dry winds the muddy pathways parch,
When to delight the dreary hours
The borders burst with David's flowers.

I say that sleepy Mother Earth
Chooses her time to bring to birth
New sprouting seeds and youngling plants
And leads the world in vernal dance.

Liz Rowlands

Why I Don't Like Roses

Plump, blousy, low-cleavage blooms,
splaying their plush petals, they invite
you into their folds with flabby, open arms.
The loud bottle-blondes, the lipstick-bright,
the roughly rouged, all spilling
bosoms and shrieking laughter. Yet,
once plucked, they soon let themselves go,
are quick to droop, fast to fade,
and underneath their ebullience,
their stem is spiked with spite.

Julie Stamp

Thimble

She slips the thimble onto her finger:
   it clasps her skin, clings like routine.
The needle cannot harm her;
   she cannot feel its sharpshock pain.

Her finger has helped sooth babies,
   felt for fever, wagged disapproval;
     closed her husband's eyelids,
   a final loving act.

She wonders why she has not hardened
   like the thimble,
grown a sleek protective skin
   like its sturdy dimpled gloss:

why she remains sensitive, susceptible;
   feels each prick of memory,
     each piercing loss.

Jenny Hamlett

The Christmas Present

Oh! I only wear silver, she said.
It burst out before she had thought.
She watched her small daughter's smile fall away
into the crack she'd made.

It burst out before she had thought.
She tried to say she liked it but words fled
into the crack she'd made.
How stupid to place colour above love.

She tried to say she liked it but words fled.
The gold necklace looked perfect in her palm.
How stupid to place colour above love.
How could she have hurt her daughter in this way?

The gold necklace looked perfect in her palm.
She knew it would never be the same.
How could she have hurt her daughter in this way?
Her daughter would never quite love her again.

She knew it would never be the same.
She watched her small daughter's smile fall away.
Her daughter would never quite love her again.
Oh! I only wear silver, she said.

Lem Ibbotson

A Prisoner of Form

If I sit down and try to write blank verse
I find I suffer from a secret sin
Despite intentions, sadly, for the worse
The urge to rhyme is always creeping in

Trying for a stream of consciousness
A mind-dump of the sentimental sort
Artifice intrudes, I must confess
Turning my efforts into wordy sport

Can I lay bare my heart within my lines
Without the stress that rhyming need obtains?
The filter of my intellect refines
Away the feeling, structure alone remains

Much is lost in cleaving to the norm
And thus am I the prisoner of form

Ian Campbell

Love Poem for Chris

I settled on a thought that
took a back-seat ride to yesterday,
that thought and I,
that back-space memory,
that once upon an earthly time,
reached for my hand and
led me through the shades and
then an open door.

And there we were,
two younger figures of ourselves,
two fairy-light facades of who we are,
two honest tigers in our stripes
and golden fur,
too innocent to over-milk the tea,
and do no more than hold the door
and kiss the ripples of goodbye.

And then the children came,
to decorate interiors with light and shade,
to make us realise that joy is real,
that love was more than kisses on a page,
two individuals with mirrored grace,
with equal right to be adored,
transformed old bricks and glass into a home,
made magic for us… *every* day.

That thought and I return and
settle like a feathered thing,
a lightweight ghost,
to find reality is as it was,
and ever shall divide
the good, the bad,
the present from the past,
but here's a thought, to ponder on at will,
for this is true, and I am sure:

That I would have less substance
than a shadow on a wall,
less pleasure in my every day,
less meaning, and assured free will,
to take each step, each lasting breath,
if I did not have that life with you,
and she and he combined,
for I would never feel that I
had ever lived,
if you had not been there…

…Oh you were the best of all my days*

*from 'Animals' by Frank O'Hara

Sally James

Bolton Palais Saturday Night 1960

Eighteen years old, suspenders and a sixpence,
starched petticoats swirling thigh high in a tizzy of rock.
Silver ball cascading star drops onto creme puff faces
Brylcreem hair glistening as drain-piped legs jive to the roll.
Primitive perfume intermingling with testosterone,
whilst wall flowers weep, watching eagerly, just in case.
Saturday night frolics on a cocktail of orange juice
and Woodbines as stilettos cramp pre-corn toes.
Girls aware of last minute lads, who sneak in after ten,
full of Newcastle Brown and Robinson's best bitter.
Their Senior Service breath gasping, hoping
for a bit of heaven in a last waltz smooch.

Sally Charnock

For Her....Later....

In the rain, we stood,
Unannounced, gone cold,
The make-up gone,
The eyes still there,
At that age
Too drunk to care.
With that look,
I remember her.
Then, years later,
We met again,
The eyes cold,
The youth gone,
A woman with a knowing air,
The trappings of accomplishment all there...
The man, the children, a home for her.
I keep her photograph,
Once I tried to keep her.
The secrets which we shared,
When young, did not escape the box,
But did, in age, become a weight to bear.
Now, our time is gone, like drink,
That friendship spent,
I cannot say these thoughts aloud, nor dare.
In the meanderings of my memory,
I keep a place for her.

Vicki Morley

Looks Like Strange Weather

A scullery maid scrubs new potatoes.
Dust falls with brown loam,
clings to her well-worn pattens.
Hay-dust from the stables
hangs on her petticoat.

In this corner of the Lincolnshire Wolds,
an east wind blows over the estate,
ruffling thirsty summer crops.
On top of the dairy, a rusty weather vane
groans and swivels with the gusts.

Clouds of dander rise from her master's mare.
Released from a dandy brush,
it hides in the cobbles, waits for rain.
The groom's habit breathes oat dust.
He hoists a tartan blanket over her withers.

Into this drowsy morning, a sudden
hail shower drums across the fields.
Cold flecks from unimportant places
mingle with the warm breeze,
melt in the stable yard, before –

the summer drought of 1716 bites.
Early autumn, the master rides to the city
of London. He reports the river
was so low, citizens walked
under the bridges.

Stacey Lane

Going South

Towards Buckland Tout Saints in the afternoon;
you take a rutted tractor road
with tyre prints knobbly in the mud.
Either side, hedges of holly, hawthorn, beech
shelter a few hardy winter flowerets.
A merry wind shouts tales from the sea
through the long grass of the high moor
while black sailed crows flap over it.
Clouds, yellow-tinged, trail banners across the sky.
Tranquillity nestles in an unpeopled landscape.
Then dusk draws it into the invisible.

Adrian Green

From the Cliff Gardens

Watching the ebb
as the mudflats emerge
and waders busy themselves
at the littoral edge

a curlew and the oystercatchers
call, their voices blending
strangely with the blackbirds,
tits and wagtails in the shrubs behind

      a jogger pounds the promenade
      sweating the afternoon sun

the memorial bench I'm sitting on
already commemorates
someone born later than me

but this is not
an afternoon for death
or contemplation beyond
the next tide, the next renewal
or what the afterworld may hold

      A mother pushes a buggy, her
      toddler straggles raggedly behind

it is a time for watching
the sky reflected in the pools
and streaks of estuary mud

for listening to the world,
its hum
        its hum
the never-silent rumble
from the shipping lanes.

Andrew W. Pye

Exquisite Corpses

The call-up papers called them.
The contracts that will bind.
And Death brings death upon them.
The warrants have been signed.
The Life that stretched before them.
The Life they left behind.

Their foes ahead lack kindness.
And they'll respond in kind.
The battlefields are manned now.
These battlefields are mined.
The hate they found before them.
The loves they left behind.

They lied about their ages.
Yet young brows soon are lined.
The trenches filled with trench-foot,
brass shells and orange rind.
The tragic masks before them.
The laughs they left behind.

At front-line's back are Top Brass
The chateaux where they dined.
"By Christmas it's all over.
In Berlin you'll be wined."
The brutal truths before them.
The lies they left behind.

Through mist and mustard gases
the blind will lead the blind.
In midnight fight the moon shone.
Their boots and buttons shined.
The foreign fields before them.
The land they left behind.

Denis Ahern

Turning Point

Marked as if a cross, and hard-cast in steel,
Focus and core of a constant union,
Firm-fixed amid all that may turn and wheel,
The perfect pole of a piercing pinion,
A crucial cap crowning a vital shaft,
Catalyst to an adhesion supreme,
A token of accuracy, skill, craft,
Vital to any construction scene,
Easily reversed should the need arise,
Trusty, staunch, dependable, durable,
As smart a gizmo as wit could devise,
With careful use even reusable,
Turning point, fulcrum, steady, true,
Top dead centre of a Philip's head screw.

Sylvia Armstrong

A Lifetime of Loving

The days they were painted. The time it was spring.
When we got acquainted my passionate king.
Golden your body and golden the dawn.
Bright golden flowers that scattered the lawn.
And golden the pleasure when passion was born
I threaded and threaded that bright dance with thee.
Too soon you were crossing the river with me.
Elation Creation then deep rest there could be.
If once more in the springtime you crossed it with me.

The days they were suntanned the time was mid-June.
We met in the sunlight, made love by the moon.
Silver your body and silver the day.
Bright silver the sand that stretched to the bay.
Silver the moonbeams that showed us the way
In shivering sureness I reached out to be
The one who was crossing the river with thee.
Purity security and love there could be.
If now in midsummer you crossed it with me.

The days they were tinted the time it was fall.
Our passion unstinted not faded at all.
Rainbowed your body and rainbowed the light.
Bright coloured rainbows enfolded the night
Rainbow elation as we soared to the height
In passionate pureness I longed still to see
That now you were crossing the river with me.
Emotion commotion then peace there will be.
If still in the autumn you cross it with me.

The days they were dreary the time it was cold.
But passions unweary though we are growing old
Misted your body and misted the dusk.
Muted responses reclaimed from the dust.
Pale misted heather strange scented with musk
With patient awaiting I came slowly to see.
That once more in our twilight you crossed it with me.
Sensations cessation sweet tranquillity.
For now it's for ever you have crossed it with me.

Rose Docherty

Perspectives

I shortened my step
for a black beetle scuttling
across my path. My shadow
is a passing cloud. I am
too large to see, a part
of its environment, like a tree
or a black hole. Its universe
is smaller than mine. Or perhaps
larger, at a scale I cannot see.

John Starbuck

Wmbldn

pat pat pat pat pat
whack
Ningle-Nong
pat pat pat pat pat
whack Urg!
Ningle-Hall
pat pat pat
whack!   EEurgh1
bip
Firs Lurve
pat pat
whack Eurg
Dirty-People
pat pat pat pat pat
whack!   Eeeurg!
Dirty-Floor
pat pat pat pat   pat pat pat
whack! Yerse!
Haughty-Bertie
pat pat pat twitch pat pat pat pat
whack! Eurrrgh!
Vaux!
Billinge
clap clap clap clap clapclapclap
AAAhhhhh
Train!
EEEEEEEh
clap clap clap roar whistle clap clap clap clap

Bernard Rooney

Political Tennis (Love, Labours Lost)

Brexit means Brexit
Double fault
Strong and stable government
Oh, I say!
What's Labour in the polls pet?
Forty, love.
Abolish tuition fees
Advantage Corbyn
Dianne Abbots misspoke
Deuce
I put the bins out
New balls please
Paul Nuttall blames tennis elbow
and claims his dog ate his manifesto.
You CANNOT be serious!
Plenty of spin and low lobs near the net
but not first past the post just yet
Tiebreak
As May turned to June she lost her bloom
It's game, set and match to the DUP.

Nigel Kent

Empty Nest

I found it under
the cherry tree:
a starling's nest,
abandoned by its
rowdy residents
who took their leave
two weeks before,
writing farewell
in cursive script
across the pale,
vellum sky.

In cradled fingers
I take it to the house,
and lay it by
her pile of post:
something to show
and tell when she
returns at end of term…

…which seems so
long to wait
and feelings that
I'd cased
and stored
with carrier bags
of cuddly toys
and old school books
strain the catches.

I see her, still,
standing on
the hostel steps,
half-turned,
hand raised,
and her last
whispered 'Bye'
evaporating
from the clouded glass
and remember how,
returning home,
I lost my way.

This poem has been included in *A Restricted View from Under the Hedge Number 1* (Hedgehog Press)

K. J. Barrett

The Broad Highway

The lilting voice drags me back
To the old Cork road,
The highway broad and white,
Story book heroes filling the brain,
Swirls of dust
Rise from clopping hoofs,
The caravan crawling
Along lazy lanes,
Wayside inns havens of light
In the purple dusk.

A coil of tobacco smoke
Tangles with the tinker's yarn,
The road a clot of blood
Paved with bone.
The shillelagh
I bought in Gratton Street
A rib
Hanging on the wall.

Remembering a walk from Rosslare to Cork undertaken in the early 1970s. My idealised perception of Southern Ireland forever changed.

Barbara Cumbers

Rosebay Willowherb

In the Blitz, bits of houses were piled
in grey hillocks, part-rooms hung
from gap-toothed walls, shreds of wallpaper

flapping like victory flags in small defiance.
Homes were asbestos boxes, row upon row
of flat-roofed greyness. Slowly bricks and concrete

grew from rubble like the rosebay that glowed
through every spring of my childhood.
Blocks of flats flourished in new estates,

balcony pots the only greenness
and rosebay a weed to be banished.
The prefabs have long gone. Soon

the flats too will lie piled in grey hillocks
though rosebay still grows along the railway
in thin restricted lines of survival.

Polly Stretton

Homage to Mondrian

Avant-garde minimalist, stunning,
Piet Mondrian made the running,
black, white, opposing pairs,
primary colours—oblongs, squares.
Strict Dutch Calvinist, he did his duty,
yet intuited basic forms of beauty,
a Utopian ideal, of order
and rhythm,
his paintings neat, neoplasticism,
pure abstract control freak,
his technique,
"…more or less Cubist
…more or less pictorial"
symmetry avoided. A memorial:
aesthetic balance through opposition,
driven to simplify, a man with a mission.

Eric Karoulla

woman with a niqab in a hospital waiting room

she walks past
– a ghost of fabric
and flesh – composing silent sonatas
with the swish of her ebony dress
wearing her sunlight and
jasmine on the inside

Alice Harrison

Married by the Book

In my tremulous, yearning girlhood
I worshipped a young Apollo, golden haired,
and married The Collected Poems of Rupert Brooke.

He adored my pale hair and pale hands.
He also adored raven and red heads
and often left me while he swam in the Cam with chaps.

As he matured and gained gravitas
he fired my political passions, taught me mysticism
and became The Collected Poems of W.B. Yeats.

He trod softly around my dreams
and loved my fugitive soul.
In middle age he renounced his unrequited loves.

But I grew weary of men and their masculine rhymes,
formal verse, abstract nouns, end-stopped lines:
my husband blossomed into The Collected Poems of Sylvia Plath.

At first we were impulsive and carefree.
I thought I could take on the world and her Daddy
until I was overwhelmed and then came The End.

Now I live alone
with a whole library of Collected Poems.
I can always find a one-night stand.

Jacob Lund

Aubade

There was no final reach across your sheets,
No hands that locked and unlocked on the bed:
Instead, a wine-wet kiss kept us all tight
In someone else's doorway, an unfit place
Down some side street that we half-knew; a space
That we knew well.
Close by, a bookie's light had been left on,
Red with the impossible.

And after that which had not taken place
Except in thoughts of mine,
Your family took your looks and mouth away
Towards a separate home.
I topped myself up with a hidden sneer,
Reflexive in its damage;
You touched my face and said we had to stop.

Walking home, the grey light and the amber lamps
Illuminated nothing: me. By now
You were undressed and warmed in bed,
And looked ahead and saw the kids,
The supermarket and the car,
And sequences in time beyond that dawn.

Helen Harvey
(June 1967 - September 2017)

Now, and Then

I inhabit this hour.
It's early and we are outside, drinking tea.
I admire the hedgerow, a scramble
of tall nettles and white roses
woven through with sticky buds
and studded with dainty campions.
Frogspit hangs from the stem of a bending bramble.
Clover dots the grass in tight-furled cups,
Its tripart leaves glistening with last night's rain —
a storm that saturates this morning's warmth
with a guttural, green, earthy scent
as if I were meant to imbibe life
with every lungful.
I breathe deeply, ignore the pain.

You inhabit this hour, and others:
your hours are still plenty,
your breath unmeasured, unrestricted,
so you speak of 2020,
a sumptuous mystery holiday
paid for by instalments, step by easy step
from this treasured present
to that unreachable day,
a then so clearly superimposed on now
that, as though through a hole in the hedge, I watch
you walking away along a beach
hand in hand with the next one,

the woman after me
—yes, there must be one—
into a bright and foreign sunset
and out of reach;
a then so clearly stamping its duet
across this misty, grey-clad morning
with its beautiful English summer scents
and the crows in the tree line
that I feel the crush of love's regret:
you and her a pair,
and me no longer there.

Yesterday's blooms litter the grass with white petals;
a solitary dandelion stalk stands bare,
its clock blown;
but I will inhabit this hour, not future years.
The rising sun already dries our tears.

Jim Lindop

28th June 1928

"Some say Louis set jazz free that day.

Why, he took Joe Oliver's slow-dragger -
laid-back ballroom shuffle, OK in its way,

'mindin' us all of The Big Easy's swagger,

and freaked it into somethin' no jazzman heard
before and broke our chains. Why, even Bird,
he'd say it was his high-set bar,
those openin' phrases – caviare
on a roll.
Nat Cole
played Fatha's solo till his fingers bled
and Red?
Well, Red'd tell you, when he'd heard all that,
…..then Louis' solo – high B-flat and all, his scat
duet with Jimmy Strong, he damn near quit.
They guys at Okeh just 'bout threw a fit.....

But that's all hist'ry now.
Things had to change and Louis showed us how.

Ladies and gentlemen, when it's time to choose
the day jazz turned into an art,
I reckon, from the bottom of my heart,
it was that day young Louis put down his 'West End Blues.'"

Julie Anne Gilligan

Classified Ad:
RUNNER WANTED
Opportunity of a Lifetime!

Cook and valet on the go
in any weather, sun or snow
this job provides much exercise
our client needs you to provide
him with his chosen special diet:
eggs for breakfast, poached or fried;
for lunch a platter of moussaka,
two full flagons: best retsina,
supper, cheese on toast will do
then your day is nearly through,
apart from double midnight snack
before you turn and hit the sack
if this sounds all Greek to you,
you're on track for interview
a long term post, so if you please
our client wants three referees
no fear of heights, nor wild beasts,
this job will take you to the peaks
no moss to gather ever more,
won't make you rich but never poor
and best of all the perks attached,
you'll never pay more income tax
the role is onwards, up and down
some jokes may ease his furrowed frown
so if you think this sounds like you
your CV's all you have to do
please mark your application thus:
Sisyphus @ jobsmart, Tartarus.

Sue Spiers

How I Learned to 'B'

Purse lips on balloon skin, blowsives
explode, b...b...bang, b...b...bang,
Boom-bang-a-bang, rubber bullets.
Beat it, beat-box, begin the beguine.
Baby, baby, ooh, baby, baby,
Babooshka, Kate Bush banshee,
The boys are back, back for good,
Beach Boys, Bar...Bar...Bar Bar...Barbra-Ann
Bachelor boy, being boring, bad,
Bad, bad, Leroy Brown, brown eyes blue,
Blue bayou, Ben, Billie Jean,
Being Bobby's girl, Barbie girl,
Pappa's brand new bag, black Betty.
Back to black, Blackberry way,
Balling the jack, ballroom blitz,
put the bomp in the bomp ba bomp ba bomp.
Busy, busy bee, beez in the trap.
I blame it on the boogie.

Rosa Thomas

To My Son

"I just want to look over the brow of the hill.
We haven't been down this lane before.
What is beyond the next bend in the road?
Who, do you think, lives behind that door?

Will you buy me a book about science?
I need an encyclopedia to keep.
I'll read a few pages of this travel book
before I go to sleep."

Always running before me
when your years numbered less than ten,
I struggled to find the answers
to your 'how', 'what', 'where' and 'when'.

One day, by the wisdom of nature,
it will be my turn to go on ahead
and turn that ultimate corner
where no-one can go in my stead.

A man now, your curiosity
keeps you questioning still;
but I won't be able to tell you
what lies over the brow of the hill.

Poets

Ahern, Denis	32	Kent, Nigel	38
Armstrong, Sylvia	33	Lane, Stacey	27
Barrett, K. J.	40	Lindop, Jim	48
Bones, Mark	13	Lund, Jacob	45
Campbell, Ian	22	McCaffrey, Chris	16
Charnock, Sally	25	McGivern, Ross	8
Cody, Cate	14	Mellon, Hilary	12
Craddock, Phil	9	Morley, Vicki	26
Cumbers, Barbara	41	Paingankar, Kewal	11
Docherty, Rose	35	Pye, Andrew W.	30
Durham, Alan	6	Rawlings, Katherine	7
Gilligan, Julie Anne	49	Rooney, Bernard	37
Green, Adrian	28	Rowlands, Liz	18
Hamlett, Jenny	20	Spiers, Sue	50
Harrison, Alice	44	Stamp, Julie	19
Harvey, Helen	46	Starbuck, John	36
Ibbotson, Lem	21	Stretton, Polly	42
James, Sally	24	Thomas, Rosa	51
Jarvis Bryant, Susan	15	Tromp, Onno	10
Karoulla, Eric	43	Williams, Barrie	17

www.ingramcontent.com/pod-product-compliance
Lightning Source LLC
Chambersburg PA
CBHW061300040426
42444CB00010B/2450